Our Changing World

THE TIMELINE LIBRARY

THE HISTORY OF THE CLOCK

BY BARBARA A. SOMERVILL

4000 B.C.	2000 B.C.	A.D. 0	2000	4000

THE CHILD'S WORLD® • CHANHASSEN, MINNESOTA

Published in the United States of America by The Child's World®
PO Box 326 • Chanhassen, MN 55317-0326 • 800-599-READ • www.childsworld.com

ACKNOWLEDGMENTS
The Child's World®: Mary Berendes, Publishing Director

Editorial Directions, Inc.: E. Russell Primm, Editorial Director; Katie Marsico, Associate Editor and Line Editor; Judith Shiffer, Assistant Editor; Matt Messbarger, Editorial Assistant; Susan Hindman, Copy Editor; Sarah E. De Capua, Proofreader; Peter Garnham, Olivia Nellums, Molly Symmonds, and Stephen Carl Wender, Fact Checkers; Tim Griffin/IndexServ, Indexer; Cian Loughlin O'Day, Photo Researcher; Linda S. Koutris, Photo Selector

The Design Lab: Kathleen Petelinsek, Design and Art Production

PHOTOS
Cover/frontispiece images: Hulton-Deutsch Collection/Corbis (main); Comstock/Punchstock (left inset); Casio (right inset).

Interior: Corbis: 5 (Larry Williams), 7 (Gianni Dagli Orti), 9 (Charles & Josette Lenars), 10 (Mimmo Jodice), 24 (Bettmann), 27 (Lester V. Bergman), 29 (Dave G. Houser); Getty Images: 13 (Taxi/Christoph Wilhelm), 16 (Hulton|Archive); The Granger Collection: 14, 18, 21.

Timeline: Archivo Iconografico, S.A./Corbis: 17; Bettmann/Corbis: 6, 11; Getty Images/Time Life Pictures/TIME Magazine: 25; HarperCollins: 27; NASA/JPL: 19; NATO: 26; Photodisc/Punchstock: 20; Pictures Now: 9 (William Page), 15 (Newell Convers Wyeth), 23; White House/Eric Draper: 28.

LIBRARY OF CONGRESS CATALOGING-IN-PUBLICATION DATA
Somervill, Barbara A.
  The history of the clock / By Barbara A. Somervill.
    p. cm. — (The timeline library (series))
  ISBN 1-59296-344-7
  1. Clocks and watches—Juvenile literature. I. Title. II. Our changing world series
  TS542.5.S66 2004
  681.1'13'09—dc22   2004003734

TABLE OF CONTENTS

ON TIME

T he alarm clock clicks, and loud music blasts Quincy from a deep sleep. It is 6:45 A.M. He gets up and heads for the shower.

At 7:00, Quincy grabs a quick breakfast of toast and orange juice. By 7:15, he is waiting outside for the school bus. Once in school, he listens to 15 minutes of announcements in homeroom before the first class bell rings.

Quincy's school day follows a tight schedule. After the bell comes math, science, and language arts. Another bell announces lunch at precisely 11:50. Afternoons bring three more classes before the final bell at 3:10.

Baseball practice starts at 3:30 P.M. After two hours of practice and a three-minute shower, Quincy heads home. Dinner is at 6:30, followed by a couple of hours of homework. A favorite television show comes on at 9:00, and it's lights-out at 10:00.

Students in class often spend time watching the clock.

Quincy, like most people, lives by the clock. Yet, this wasn't always so. Once, people got up with the sun. They ate when they were hungry—not when the clock said to eat. At sundown, people went to bed. How did the clock become so important in daily life?

CHAPTER ONE

WHY TELL TIME?

P eople did not wake up one day and ask, "What time is it?" At first, time was not seconds, minutes, and hours. Days of the week and months of the year did not exist.

Early humans noted sunrise and sunset and the passing of seasons. Life revolved around food. People rose with the sun and hunted for food. They ate when they had food—not according to a three-meals-per-day schedule.

Perhaps 20,000 years ago, an early human scratched a mark on a cave wall for every full moon. Perhaps that clever caveman noticed that three moons passed when plants had new growth. Another three moons passed, fruit ripened, and game was plentiful. Then came three moons for collecting nuts and drying meat. If humans didn't collect enough food, the next three cold moons brought great hunger.

18,000 B.C.

Humans record passage
of time on cave walls.

Hunter-gatherer clans slowly
move across North America.

3000 B.C.: CALENDARS

One of the first advances in timekeeping was the calendar. Five thousand years ago, the Sumerians of the Tigris-Euphrates Valley (present-day Iraq) developed a calendar with twelve thirty-day parts—months— per year. Each Sumerian day was made up of twelve units, roughly equal to two of our hours. The twelve units

ca. 8000 B.C.

The bow and arrow are invented at around this time.

Five thousand years ago, the Sumerians developed a calendar much like the one we use today.

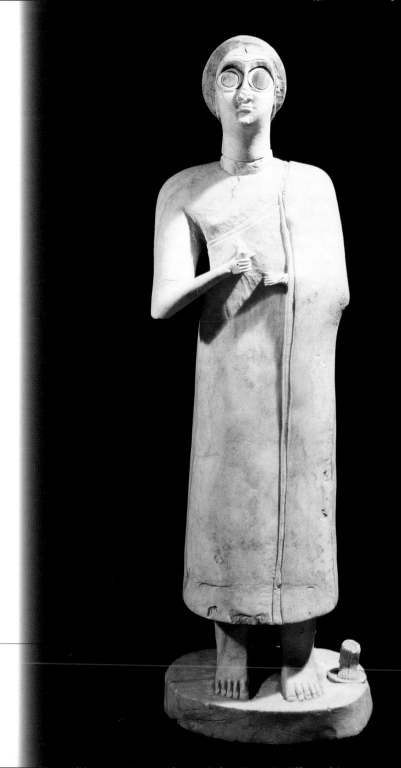

were further divided into thirty smaller periods, about four of our minutes.

In Egypt, scientists noted that Sirius, the "dog star," rose close to the sun every 365 days. This event marked the life-giving flooding of the Nile River. It started each new year for Egyptians. The Egyptian 365-day calendar dates back to 4236 B.C.

In what is now Central America, the Mayans developed a two-calendar society. The Mayan sun-based calendar marked daily events, such as planting, hunting, or harvesting. The moon-based calendar set religious events. The Mayans believed that the world began in what is now called the year 3113 B.C.

4236 B.C. — Egyptians begin using a 365-day calendar.

4000 B.C. — Plows pulled by oxen are used in farming.

3113 B.C. — According to Mayan calendars, the world is created.

3000 B.C.: SHADOWS AND SUNDIALS

One of the earliest instruments for telling time was a shadow stick. A flat board was marked with hours from dawn to sunset. In the middle of the stick, the timekeeper placed a marker shaped like a soccer goal. As the sun moved, the marker cast a shadow on the stick. The shadow's line showed the time of day. Shadow sticks worked only in daylight.

An ancient form of clock—the sundial— came along in about 3000 B.C. These were very simple-a straight stick and a dial of some sort. The earliest sundials indicated only morning,

The Mayas schedule followed a moon-based or lunar calendar for religious ceremonies.

3000 B.C.

Sumerians develop a calendar with 30 days per month.

The city of Athens (left) is founded.

9

noon, and afternoon. As the name *sundial* says, these were sun clocks. Sundials were common in Arabia, Babylonia, Egypt, Rome, and Greece. Early sundials also told time in China and Japan.

The basic parts of a sundial are the dial and the gnomon. A gnomon is the pointer that marks the sun's shadow on the dial's face. There were difficulties with telling time by sundial though. One difficulty was, of course, that no sun meant no time.

DID YOU KNOW?
IN ANCIENT EGYPT, PEOPLE HAD TRAVELING SUNDIALS. THEY WERE SMALL ENOUGH TO HOLD IN A PERSON'S HAND.

IF SOMEONE AIMED THE SUNDIAL TO THE NORTH, THAT PERSON COULD READ THE TIME!

2000 B.C.

Cuneiform is widespread across the Middle East.

This sundial told time for Romans in the 6th century B.C.

CHAPTER TWO
EARLY CLOCKS

E very clock has certain basic parts. One part marks equal segments of time. This part can be just about any shape. Time segments may be minutes, hours, days, months, or years. A clock tracks passing time and shows the results.

In ancient times, every culture had its own way of telling time. Some people, such as Babylonians and Egyptians, marked the passage of hours. The Vikings lived by the sea and measured time by the tides. People developed basic clocks, but the clocks worked on different time frames. And they were not very accurate.

300 B.C.: HOURS

As cultures became more complex, people needed better timekeeping. The Egyptians marked passing time in units, much like hours. Egyptian hours were

Babylonians divide days into 24 equal hours.

Euclid (right) develops geometry in Greece.

300 B.C.

not all the same length. Winter hours were shorter than summer hours.

In 300 B.C., the Babylonians—also from present-day Iraq—began dividing days into 24 equal parts. Every hour was the same length. Day and night hours, winter and summer hours, took up the same amount of time. The mechanical clock, invented about 1,600 years later, would make this idea of equal hours a reality.

Up to this point, timekeeping was limited to large units: years, months, days, and hours. At about this time, the Greeks invented hourglasses. A sandglass allowed the Greeks to measure parts of an hour. This was progress!

230 B.C.

Oil lamps begin to be produced in Greece.

An hourglass can tell time by minutes, hours, days, and even weeks.

The Egyptians used water clocks such as this one to mark the passage of nighttime.

A.D. 100–500: WATER CLOCKS

In about 1500 B.C., an Egyptian developed a clock that did not depend on sunshine. It was a water clock, which kept time day or night.

The Greeks called a water clock called a *clepsydra*—or "water thief." What a great name! That is exactly what a water clock does: it tells time by stealing away the water. Some water clocks consisted of water in a bowl that had hours marked on the inside wall. A tiny hole in the base of the bowl allowed water to drip out slowly. As the water dripped away, it revealed the hour marks.

By A.D. 100–500, water clocks went way beyond

A.D. 100–500

Clock makers create basic mechanical, water-run clocks.

The Anasazi culture begins to flourish in southwestern North America.

The bead and wire abacus (left) is first used in Egypt.

dripping bowls. Clock makers developed water clocks with moving figures, gongs, and bells. In 1088, Su Sung, a Chinese clock maker, built a huge water clock 30 feet (10 meters) high. The top featured a spinning globe. Moving water forced carved figures to dance past windows. Bells and gongs chimed the hour. Clocks got bigger and more complicated. They became a source of entertainment as much as a timepiece.

Other forms of early clocks included hourglasses, candle clocks, and **incense** clocks. Hourglasses or sand clocks allowed people to measure small time periods. Similar sand clocks are used today to cook three-minute eggs. Candle clocks and incense clocks depended on burning away

FOCUS ON CANDLE CLOCKS
IN ABOUT A.D. 878, PEOPLE BEGAN USING CANDLE CLOCKS. THE CANDLE HAD HOURS MARKED ON THE SIDE. AS THE CANDLE BURNED DOWN, ITS LEVEL SHOWED THE HOURS THAT HAD PASSED. HISTORIANS CREDIT ALFRED THE GREAT, KING OF WESSEX (ENGLAND), WITH INVENTING THE CANDLE CLOCK.

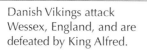

Alfred the Great develops candle clocks.

Danish Vikings attack Wessex, England, and are defeated by King Alfred.

878

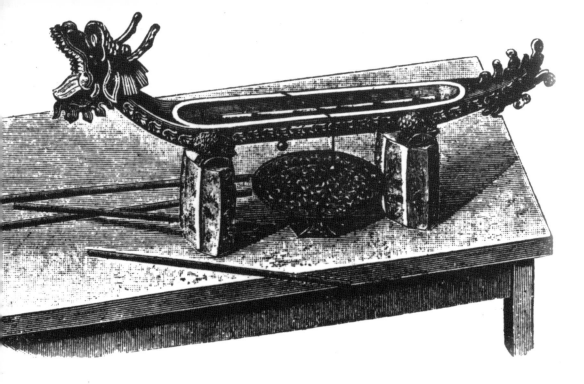

This Chinese candle clock told time as the candle burned away.

material at an even rate. As wax or incense burned away, the remaining level marked the time.

Early clocks were never accurate by today's standards. Time changed according to the seasons. Some people measured hours—which lasted different lengths depending on the culture. Others measured the passing of tides. It didn't really matter. Most people still lived by the sun up–sun down mode and didn't care what time it was. Those concerns would come much later.

1088

Su Sung builds a complex water clock in China.

A magnetic needle compass is developed.

CHAPTER THREE

MECHANICAL CLOCKS

As civilizations became more complex, people needed a better way to tell time. By the early 1300s, Italian cities began to put huge clocks in town towers. These clocks were mechanical, driven by weights and gears.

Everyone in the town lived by the same time. Few people owned personal clocks, and watches had not been invented. Unfortunately, early mechanical clocks were no more exact than water clocks or sundials.

The first major breakthrough in mechanical clocks came in 1510. Peter Henlein, a German, experimented with using springs to power clocks. The springs allowed clocks to be smaller and weigh less. As the spring wound down, the clocks ran slower. These spring-powered clocks also had

Peter Henlein experiments with using springs to power clocks.

Wallpaper is first used to decorate homes.

problems with correct timekeeping.

In 1581, the Italian scientist Galileo Galilei began experimenting with the **pendulum.** He had noticed that oil lamps in church swung at an even pace. Could a swinging pendulum regulate a clock evenly? About 60 years later, Galileo designed a pendulum clock. He died before it could be built and tested.

1657: CHRISTIAN HUYGENS

Dutch scientist Christian Huygens put Galileo's ideas to work in 1657. He designed a pendulum clock. He hired a clock maker to build the first model.

> **GALILEO GALILEI**
> GALILEO IS CONSIDERED THE
> FATHER OF MODERN PHYSICS
> AND ASTRONOMY. HE BUILT THE
> FIRST-KNOWN THERMOMETER
> AND ONE OF THE EARLIEST
> MICROSCOPES. HE ALSO BUILT A
> TELESCOPE TO STUDY THE STARS
> AND PLANETS.

Galileo died before he could test a model of his pendulum clock.

1581
Galileo Galilei experiments with the pendulum, which leads to more accurate clocks.

Elizabeth I is queen of England.

1657
Christian Huygens invents a working pendulum clock.

The first fountain pen is manufactured.

One kind of pendulum clock was the longcase clock. Later on they were called grandfather clocks. The clock consisted of a face (dial), hands, gears, and a falling weight to drive the gears. Clock makers began adding chimes and bells to longcase clocks. Bells chimed the hour, half hour, and quarter hour. Longcase clocks were expensive, so only wealthy people owned them.

Huygens continued experimenting with timekeeping. Longcase clocks were great, but they were not movable. Huygens developed a smaller clock that used a spiral spring in place of a pendulum. He received a **patent** for a pocket watch in 1675, although he was not the first to invent pocket watches.

FOCUS ON CLOCKS
IN 1999, A CLOCK SOLD FOR THE RECORD-BREAKING PRICE OF $3,001,294. THE LOUIS XVI CLOCK WAS MORE THAN 200 YEARS OLD AND INDICATED SECONDS, MINUTES, HOURS, SUNRISE AND SUNSET, THE PHASE OF THE MOON, THE DATE, AND THE DAY OF THE WEEK.

1675

Huygens patents a pocket watch.

Giovanni Cassini discovers that Saturn has multiple rings.

1776: THE LONGITUDE PRIZE

In the 1700s, a baffling problem faced the scientific world. When at sea and far from land, how could a sailor tell where his ship was? Today, this sounds silly, but in the 1700s, hundreds of ships wrecked because of this problem. Thousands of sailors lost their lives, and millions of dollars of cargo sank into the sea.

In 1714, the British government passed the **Longitude** Act. They offered a prize of 20,000 British pounds (about $1 million today) to anyone who could solve the longitude problem.

John Harrison, a carpenter's son, heard about the Longitude Prize in 1726. He began designing a device

1700s

Longitude problem baffles scientists and sailors.

Bartolomeo Cristaforo invents the piano.

that would keep accurate time while on a moving ship. Knowing how long a ship traveled and in what direction helped determine the longitude reached. Harrison's idea worked. Still, it took him 50 years and five model watches before he received the prize. By then, Harrison was 80 years old.

Patriot leaders sign the Declaration of Independence.

It took John Harrison 50 years to collect his prize for creating this marine chronometer.

CHAPTER FOUR

FROM TICK-TOCK TO SOLAR POWER

By the late 1700s, timepieces kept accurate time. Yet, problems with telling time still existed. Every town went by local "sun time." When noon struck in Elm City, the time might be11:58 in Oakville, 25 miles (40 kilometers) to the west. Each locality could say what time standard it wanted to observe.

Using "sun time" was not a big problem until trains made travel quicker. Once people could travel 100 miles (160 km) a day, using lots of local times became confusing. One train route passed through dozens of different "sun times."

On November 18, 1883, the problem was solved. The United States started using four specific time zones. Those same time zones—Eastern, Central, Mountain, and Pacific—are still in use today.

1883

The United States sets
four specific time zones.

Saltwater taffy is sold for
the first time.

1900s: TIME CHANGES

Clock makers began experimenting with electric clocks in the early 1840s. A battery provided electric pulses to power the clock. By 1916, clocks could be plugged into wall sockets. Electric clocks became cheaper, and most homes had at least one.

For many years, men had worn their watches in their trouser pocket or in their vest pocket. Women wore watches in a variety of ways, such as around their necks or pinned to their waists. Beginning around 1900, a new idea became all the rage—the wristwatch! These watches all had small pins that the owner turned to wind the watch.

In 1923, John Harwood of London, England,

DAYLIGHT SAVING TIME
THE IDEA FOR DAYLIGHT SAVING TIME FIRST CAME FROM BENJAMIN FRANKLIN IN 1784. FRANKLIN'S IDEA WAS NOT USED UNTIL WORLD WAR I (1914–1918). DAYLIGHT SAVING TIME WAS MEANT TO SAVE POWER RESOURCES AND WAS CALLED "WAR TIME."

1916

Electric-powered clocks become available.

World War I (left) continues; the United States joins the war a year later.

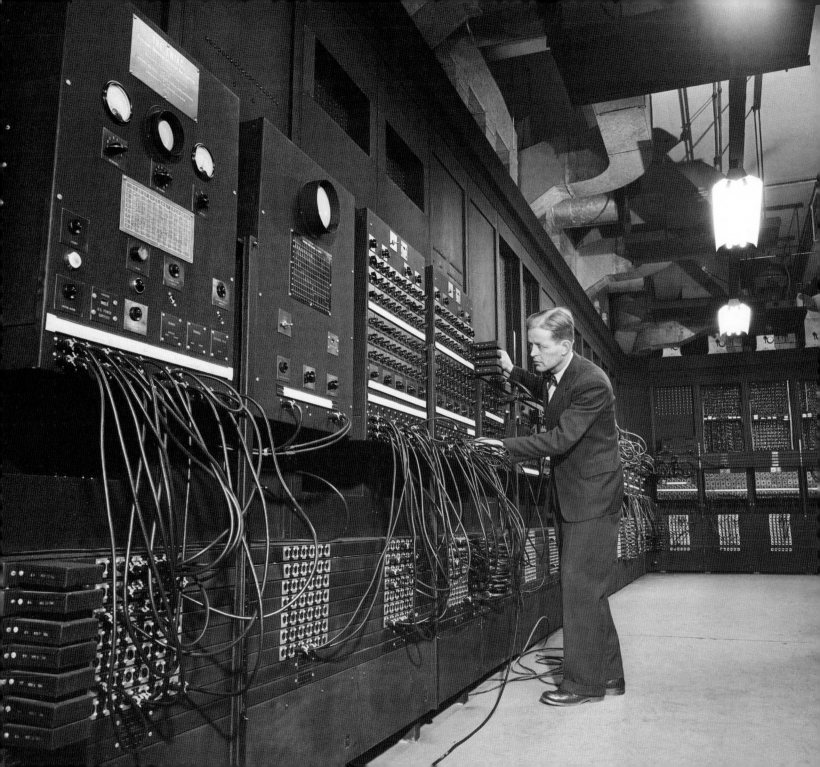

designed a wristwatch that wound itself. Over the next 50 years, watchmaking changed dramatically. Self-winding wristwatches are still popular today. Other watch advances included battery-powered watches and solar-powered watches.

When computers were invented, clocks changed forever. In 1946, the first practical computer, ENIAC, filled a room the size of a classroom. By the 1990s, computers fit easily into the watches people wore on their wrists. The tiny computers actually performed more functions than ENIAC. With an internal computer, watches had alarms, worked as stopwatches, and performed math. They told the day, month, year, and date. They even told the time!

FOCUS ON ALARM CLOCKS LEVI HUTCHINS OF NEW HAMPSHIRE INVENTED THE FIRST AMERICAN ALARM CLOCK IN 1787. FROM THEN ON, CLOCK MAKERS EXPERIMENTED WITH GONGS, CHIMES, AND BUZZERS TO WAKE SLEEPERS. SNOOZE-ALARMS DIDN'T COME ALONG UNTIL 1956, AND TODAY, FEW ALARM CLOCKS ARE MADE WITHOUT A SNOOZE FEATURE.

1923

John Harwood receives a patent for a self-winding wristwatch.

Time magazine (right) begins publishing.

1956

Snooze alarms give people an extra ten minutes rest.

Elvis Presley tops the charts with "Heartbreak Hotel."

ENIAC took up plenty of space compared to today's computers that fit inside a watch.

CHAPTER FIVE

TODAY'S TIMEPIECES

Ten thousand years ago, time was measured by seasons. One thousand years ago, hours made a difference. One hundred years ago, time zones were still a new fangled idea. Today, atomic clocks measure time to the microsecond.

Scientists began experimenting with atomic clocks in the 1930s and 1940s. In 1949, the National Institute of Standards and Technology (NIST) built the first true atomic clock. This clock was based on ammonia **molecules**—yes, the same stuff your parents use to clean the kitchen floor.

Radio-controlled clocks are a type of clock that keeps time based on atomic clocks. They look like normal clocks and cost about the same price. The value of both an atomic clock and a radio-controlled clock lies in how

1949

The first atomic clock is developed.

The North Atlantic Treaty Organization (NATO) is established (right).

accurately they keep time. Radio-controlled clocks receive radio time signals based on the time of NIST's atomic clocks. The signal adjusts the time reading. The signal corrects problems from power outages, changes in time zones, and daylight saving time.

In 1967, **cesium** became the international standard for atomic clocks. The new standard keeps time accurately to 30 billionths of a second per year.

Regardless of the power source—from gears to electricity—watches remained basically the same. They all had dials and hands-hour, minute, and second. That changed in 1970 with the invention of liquid crystal displays (**LCD**). Today, LCDs are so common that many

The radioactive element cesium is the international standard for atomic clocks.

1967	Cesium becomes the international time standard.		1970	George Gray develops a cheap, practical liquid crystal display.

Ten million children receive a new vaccine for measles.

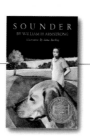

William Armstrong's *Sounder* (left) wins the Newberry Medal.

young people cannot read a standard clock.

2000: FORWARD AND BACKWARD IN TIME

Clocks come in all shapes, sizes, and styles—from cats and dogs to Uncle Sam. These clocks are usually electric or battery-powered. They decorate walls, churches, towers, and libraries. Telling time with these clocks is simple.

LCD and light-emitting diodes (**LED**) flash the time in clear, readable numbers. Timepieces with LCD and LED **digital** displays appear on signs, buildings, and watches. Hardly a bedroom, kitchen, or wrist goes without some type of timepiece.

And yet, while time has passed, the appeal of old-fashioned timekeeping has not. Antique grandfather

2001

Samsung offers a wristwatch/ telephone for sale.

George W. Bush (right) becomes president of the United States.

clocks are passed from parents to children. Clock towers throughout the world chime the hour, reminding us that time is on the move. The bizarre movements of cuckoo clocks delight some and annoy others.

Modern sundials add precision to an ancient method of telling time. Human sun clocks use a person's shadow to indicate the hour. Water clocks, shadow clocks, candle clocks—they can all still tell time.

The next time the alarm clock goes off, think about time. Does time control your life? You might just roll over . . . hit the snooze button. Sleep makes losing another five minutes worthwhile. Or does it?

Modern sundials improve an ancient style of timekeeping.

2001

The United States invades Iraq.

Cuckoo clocks such as this one provide entertainment and tell the time.

cesium (SEE-zee-uhm) Cesium is a radioactive element. In 1967, cesium became the international standard for atomic clocks.

digital (DIJ-uh-tuhl) Digital describes something that is shown, used, or developed through numbers. Timepieces with LCD and LED digital displays appear on signs, buildings, and watches.

incense (IN-senss) Incense is a substance that gives off a scent when burned. Early clocks included hourglasses, candle clocks, and incense clocks.

LCD (ELL-cee-dee) LCD stands for liquid crystal display; an LCD reacts to light and produces bright colors. LCD was invented in 1970.

LED (ELL-ee-dee) LED stands for light emitting diode; an LED produces its own light, as with a television. You can view LED digital displays on some signs, buildings, and watches.

longitude (LON-juh-tood) Longitude is a set of imaginary lines that run north to south through the poles on a globe or map. The British government offered a prize of 20,000 British pounds to anyone who could solve the longitude problem.

molecules (MOL-uh-kyoolz) Molecules are the smallest particles of a substance that cannot be divided further without changing the substance. The 1949 atomic clock was based on ammonia molecules.

patent (PAT-uhnt) A patent is a piece of paper from the government that gives a person or company the rights to make or sell a new invention. Christian Huygens received a patent for a pocket watch in 1675.

pendulum (PEN-dyuh-luhm) A pendulum is a weight hung from a fixed point so that it can swing freely. In 1581, the Italian scientist Galileo Galilei began experimenting with the pendulum.

FOR FURTHER INFORMATION

AT THE LIBRARY

Nonfiction

* Boerst, William J. *Galileo Galilei and the Science of Motion*. Greensboro, N.C.: Morgan Reynolds, 2003.

Duffy, Trent. *Turning Point Inventions: Clock*. New York: Atheneum, 2000.

Mitchell, Judy, editor. *It's About Time: Creative Activities about Time*. Carthage, Ill.: Teaching & Learning Company, 1997.

Skurzynski, Gloria. *On Time: From Seasons to Split Seconds*. Washington, D.C.: National Geographic, 2000.

* Sobel, Dava, and William J. H. Andrews. *The Illustrated Longitude*. New York: Walker Publishing, 1995.

Fiction

Dickinson, Peter. *Time and the Clock Mice*. New York: Delacorte Books for Young Readers, 1994.

* Books marked with a star are challenge reading material for those reading above grade level.

ON THE WEB

Visit our home page for lots of links about clocks: *http://www.childsworld.com/links.html*

Note to Parents, Teachers, and Librarians: We routinely check our Web links to make sure they're safe, active sites—so encourage your readers to check them out!

PLACES TO VISIT OR CONTACT

American Clock and Watch Museum
100 Maple Street
Bristol, CT 06010
860/583-6070

The Canadian Clock Museum
PO Box 1684
60 James Street
Deep River, Ontario,
Canada K0J 1P0
e-mail: enquiries@canclockmuseum.ca

The National Watch and Clock Museum
514 Poplar Street
Columbia, PA 17512-2130
717/684-8261

INDEX

ABOUT THE AUTHOR

Barbara A. Somervill is the author of many books for children. She loves learning and sees every writing project as a chance to learn new information or gain a new understanding. Ms. Somervill grew up in New York State, but has also lived in Toronto, Canada; Canberra, Australia; California; and South Carolina. She currently lives with her husband in Simpsonville, South Carolina.